Life in Medieval Europe

The City in Medieval Europe

Danielle Watson

Cavendish Square
New York

A portion of the material in this book has been derived from *Everyday Life in Medieval Europe* by Kathryn Hinds.

Published in 2017 by Cavendish Square Publishing, LLC
243 5th Avenue, Suite 136, New York, NY 10016

First Edition

CPSIA Compliance Information: Batch #CS16CSQ

All websites were available and accurate when this book was sent to press.

Library of Congress Cataloging-in-Publication Data

Names: Watson, Danielle, 1978-
Title: The city in medieval Europe / Danielle Watson.
Description: New York : Cavendish Square Publishing, 2017. |
Series: Life in medieval Europe | Includes bibliographical references and index. |
Description based on print version record and CIP data provided by
publisher; resource not viewed.
Identifiers: LCCN 2015050994 (print) | LCCN 2015049114 (ebook) |
ISBN 9781502618818 (ebook) | ISBN 9781502618801 (library bound)
Subjects: LCSH: Cities and towns, Medieval--Europe--Juvenile literature. |
City and town life--Europe--History--To 1500--Juvenile literature. |
Europe--History--476-1492--Juvenile literature. | Europe--Social life and
customs--Juvenile literature.
Classification: LCC D134 (print) | LCC D134 .W38 2017 (ebook) |
DDC 940.1--dc23
LC record available at http://lccn.loc.gov/2015050994

Editorial Director: David McNamara
Editor: Kelly Spence
Copy Editor: Nathan Heidelberger
Art Director: Jeffrey Talbot
Designer: Joseph Macri
Production Assistant: Karol Szymczuk
Photo Research: J8 Media

The photographs in this book are used by permission and through the courtesy of: MaryAnne Nelson/Moment/Getty Images, cover; Universal History Archive/UIG via Getty Images, 6; Universal History Archive/UIG via Getty Images, 4; Menno Schaefer/Shutterstock.com, 9; Unknown/File:Louvre - Les Très Riches Heures.jpg/Wikimedia Commons, 11; Gaspar van Wittel/File:Gaspar van Wittel - View of the San Marco Basin.JPG/Wikimedia Commons, 10; © North Wind Picture Archives, 12; Francesco Hayez/File:Francesco Hayez 010.jpg/Wikimedia Commons, 16; Photo12/UIG/Getty Images, 18; Olgysha/Shutterstock.com, 20; unknown master (book scan)/File:11-alimenti,carni ovine,Taccuino Sanitatis, Casanatense 4182.jpg/Wikimedia Commons, 23; Leemage/UIG via Getty Images, 25; Scirocco340/Shutterstock.com, 28; © British Library Board/Bridgeman Images, 31; NYPL NYPL/Science Source/ Getty Images, 33; DeAgostini/Getty Images, 34; Ann Ronan Pictures/Print Collector/Getty Images, 37; Universal History Archive/Getty Images, 39; mandritoiu/Shutterstock.com, 40; © Tallandier/Bridgeman Images, 42; © PVDE/Bridgeman Images, 44; Bibliotheque Nationale, Paris, France/Bridgeman Images, 46; Art Media/Print Collector/Getty Images, 51; Fine Art Images/Heritage Images/Getty Images, 49; Hulton Archive/Getty Images, 54; © Lebrecht Music and Arts Photo Library/Alamy Stock Photo, 57; © British Library Board/Bridgeman Images, 60; Leemage/UIG via Getty Images, 62; © Heritage Image Partnership Ltd/Alamy Stock Photo, 64; Bridgeman Images, 66.

Printed in the United States of America

Contents

Introduction

The Medieval Age

The Italian city of Siena was an important center of commerce during the thirteenth century.

The medieval period, also known as the Middle Ages, spans about one thousand years of European history, between 500 and 1500. The years 1100–1400 made up the High Middle Ages, a period distinguished by a swelling population that led to great social, economic, and political changes across the continent.

The late Middle Ages saw the emergence of **humanists**, individuals who, during the fourteenth century, took a renewed interest in ancient Roman and Greek literature and ideologies. Humanists believed that the previous ten centuries had been a dark age, with no great human advancements or thinkers. They sought to distance themselves from this time period and to create a rebirth of ancient learning. The rise of humanism led to the period following the Middle Ages, which became known as the Renaissance.

As the Middle Ages progressed, great cities were founded across Europe. Some grew as centers of trade and commerce, while others flourished around elaborate churches or walled fortresses. Still more became centers of thriving industry and education, with the scholarly pursuit of knowledge leading to the emergence of the world's first universities. Thousands of people flocked to these vibrant urban centers to practice their trades and buy and sell their wares in the narrow streets and crowded squares. With this growing swell of people, a new middle class of merchants and craftspeople was born, giving way to a new chapter in European history.

Chapter One

The Rise of the Medieval City

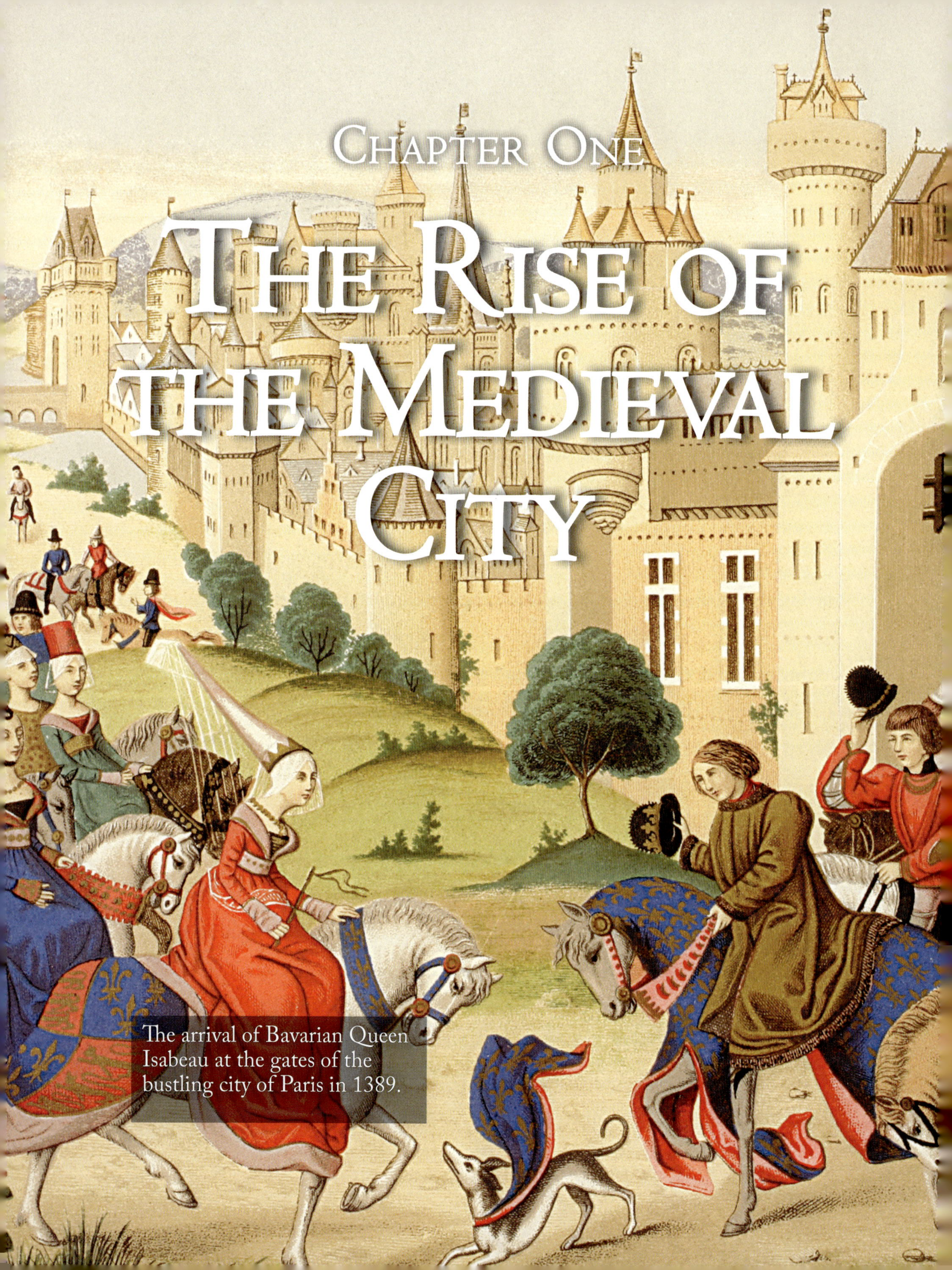

The arrival of Bavarian Queen Isabeau at the gates of the bustling city of Paris in 1389.

"The University, a solid mass of slated roofs, covered the left bank of the Seine from the Tournelle to the tower of Nesle and spread over the hill of St. Genevieve; the Cite, with its twenty-one churches, covered the island of the Cite, and the Ville covered the right bank with its gardens and palaces. Around this city of a thousand churches I and ten thousand houses, all fused and huddled together as if for warmth and protection, were the stray towers and windmills of the suburbs."

—a description of medieval Paris in 1456, based on the works of the fifteenth-century poet Francois Villon

Long before the Middles Ages, the city of Rome had been established in 753 BCE. This ancient city served as the seat of the mighty Roman Empire. As the empire gained new lands and stretched farther across Europe, many Roman cities were founded. These cities served as hubs of urban life until the fall of the Roman Empire in 476 CE.

With the end of Roman rule, several of these cities fell into decay. Constant warfare brought trade—the lifeblood of cities—almost to a halt. Particularly in northwest Europe, rural life grew in importance as power was concentrated in the hands of large landowners. Local farming was the cornerstone of the economy. Most areas produced only what they needed; there was rarely a surplus of food or goods that could be traded.

The Roman cities that survived—such as Paris (France) and Cologne (Germany)—were often those where a **bishop** was headquartered. A bishop was a high-ranking Christian priest who oversaw religious affairs for a particular region. His church was called a **cathedral**. For some time, however, even a cathedral city might be composed of only sixty to eighty small houses, and most of the city's area might still be gardens, orchards, and pastures.

At first the situation was better for cities in what is now southern France, on the Mediterranean coast. Marseilles and other towns continued to do business with the ports of the eastern Mediterranean. This trade, too, was interrupted when Muslim warriors swept through the Mediterranean world in the seventh and eighth centuries. These warriors were filled with enthusiasm to spread the religion of **Islam**. Soon ancient cities such as Alexandria (Egypt) and Córdoba (Spain) again flourished, this time under Muslim rule. The followers of Islam also established thriving new cities, including Cairo (Egypt) and Baghdad (Iraq). During this period, the only really great Christian city was Constantinople (now Istanbul, Turkey), the center of the wealthy Byzantine Empire. The Byzantine Empire was the successor of the eastern half of the ancient Roman Empire. Its core was Asia Minor and Greece, and its culture was quite different from that of the rest of medieval Europe.

Slowly, however, cities began to make a comeback in northwest Europe. The sixth and seventh centuries saw the spread of Christian **monasteries**, highly organized communities devoted to religious life. Craftspeople, merchants, and farmers were quick to gather around the monasteries. Some of these monastic centers eventually grew into true cities. For example, Germany's "Monks' Town" became the thriving city of Munich.

All of these upheavals had limited effect on northern Italy. Here, without interruption, city life continued to be of great importance. Milan, Florence,

The ruins of Lindisfarne, the site of the first Viking raid in Britain in 793 CE.

The Viking Raids

By the ninth century, trade was reviving. Cities such as Dorestad, in what is now the Netherlands, became bustling centers of trade. The wealth and prosperity of Dorestad and similar cities attracted Viking raiders, who traveled to Europe from Scandinavia, the region that makes up modern-day Norway, Denmark, Finland, and Sweden. As a seafaring people, the Vikings sailed to northern Europe aboard shallow-bottomed longboats, which could travel speedily across the open sea and up rivers.

Thus, many coastal and riverside settlements suffered heavily from Viking attacks. However, towns also strengthened their fortifications as a result of the Viking raids, and many fortresses built as defenses against the Vikings soon grew into cities. The Vikings themselves founded a number of new cities, and not only in their Scandinavian homeland: for example, Dublin was one of many Irish cities established by the Vikings.

Pisa, Bologna, Verona, Padua, and Genoa had all been well-established urban communities since Roman times or even earlier. Rome itself, "the eternal city," maintained a special place in European culture, for its bishop, the pope, was the head of the Catholic Church of western Europe.

One major Italian city did not have its origin in the Roman Empire but actually arose during the Middle Ages. This was Venice, founded in 697 by the union of several communities built on marshy islands just off the northeast coast of Italy. Within a few centuries, Venice was a great power in the Mediterranean, and by 1201 it was the trading capital of Europe.

Many of today's capitals were founded during the High Middle Ages; in the west, Belfast (Ireland); to the north, Amsterdam (Netherlands) and Copenhagen (Denmark); and to the east, Berlin (Germany). Whether old or new, these cities became important centers for trade and culture in medieval Europe.

Boats fill the canals of Venice, an Italian city located at the top of the Adriatic Sea.

During the Middle Ages, the Louvre stood as a feudal fortress in the heart of Paris.

Europe's Largest Cities

By modern standards, medieval cities had rather small populations. However, an average country village of the time had only from 150 to 250 residents. In comparison, the cities were very heavily populated.

Here are western Europe's largest cities around the year 1250, ranked by approximate population:

80,000–100,000: Venice (Italy)

50,000 to 100,000: Genoa and Milan (Italy)

50,000: Paris (France); Bologna and Palermo (Italy)

40,000: Ghent (Flanders—now Belgium)

25,000: London (England); Marseilles, Toulouse, Lille, and Rouen (France); Florence and Naples (Italy)

10,000: York (England); Barcelona and Seville (Spain); Troyes and Montpellier (France); Cologne (Germany); and many others

Chapter Two

Governing a City

A member of the clergy collects taxes from merchants at a market in Tournay, France, during the fourteenth century.

"The place of the head in the body of the commonwealth is filled by the prince … The place of the heart is filled by the senate … The duties of eyes, ears, and tongues are claimed by the judges and governors of provinces. Officials and soldiers correspond to the hands … Financial officers … may be compared with the stomach and intestines …"
—John of Salisbury, *Policraticus* (*The Stateman's Book*), twelfth century

Many medieval cities were ruled by members of the nobility. As kings and lords amassed more land and their rule spread across greater distances, cities provided a central location from which to run their governments. This led to the birth of capital cities in Europe. Governing a city also fattened its ruler's coffers; kings and lords profited greatly by collecting taxes on goods that moved in and out of a city, fines from the courts, and rent from buildings held under city ownership or control.

Royal control benefited townspeople, too. People who lived in a royal city were automatically free from serfdom: they were not required to work on a lord's land or pay the many fees that **serfs** owed their lords. In some parts of Europe, a serf could become free simply by moving to a city and living there for a year and a day.

A number of cities were under the rule of a count or other lord, who was usually a royal **vassal**. The French city of Troyes was ruled by the count of Champagne, a vassal of the king of France. The count received the same taxes, fines, and rents that royal cities paid to the king. Often both kings and counts encouraged trade and prosperity by guaranteeing protection for merchants traveling to the cities under their control.

In northern and central Italy, it was not unusual for cities to have nothing to do with royalty at all. Officially, most of them were ruled by the Holy Roman emperor, but in practice, many were countries in their own right. Some powerful cities also controlled other cities, along with rural areas.

These city-states were governed in various ways. For example, during the twelfth century, many places hired a professional administrator, called a podesta, to run the city for a certain amount of time. Usually the podesta was from another region so that he could not be easily swayed by any of the different factions in the town he was overseeing. Other cities, such as Florence and Venice, were republics, where government officials were elected. During the thirteenth and fourteenth centuries, some Italian city-states came to be ruled by independent dukes. These dukedoms usually became hereditary; for example, the dukes of Milan came from the Visconti family, and those of Ferrara from the Este family.

The Great Republic of Venice

The greatest medieval republic was the city of Venice. Its government evolved slowly over many centuries, taking its final form in the years from 1297 to 1310.

A duke, called the doge (dohj), was the head of state. His actual powers were quite limited, but he had great influence and prestige. His presence was required at every meeting of each branch of the government. Six dogal councillors assisted him and made certain that he did not try to increase his authority. Three councillors were elected at a time, and they remained in office for only eight months. Together the doge, the dogal councillors, and the city's three chief judges fulfilled such duties as overseeing elections and making recommendations to the Senate.

The Senate was a body of 120 men, each elected for a one-year term, plus as many as 155 other officials. Some of these officials had the right to vote in the Senate, but others did not. The Senate dealt with foreign affairs, finances, trade policies, and other issues. It levied taxes and customs duties, declared war, and made the laws of the republic.

The senators and most other government officials were chosen by the Great Council. This council was made up of all Venetian noblemen aged twenty-five and above. Besides electing senators, judges, admirals, ambassadors, provincial governors, the doge, and others, the Great Council also debated political issues and approved the decisions of the Senate.

The members of the Great Council were under constant scrutiny by the Council of Ten. This group was formed in 1310 to protect the republic from enemies both outside and within the city. The ten councillors were elected for one-year terms by the Venetian government. They saw that swift and ruthless punishment was dealt to any noble who abused his position, conspired to overthrow Venice's government, or plotted with foreign powers. The Council of Ten's authority was held in check by the Great Council, which could, if necessary, refuse to elect anyone to the Council of Ten.

The common people of Venice had little say in their government's decisions. However, during the Middle Ages, they would gather in the city's main square to voice their approval or disapproval of the government's

This painting shows Doge Marino Faliero in the final moments before his execution. He was sentenced to death as punishment for leading a plot against the ruling patricians.

actions. The election of the doge also had to be ratified by the assembled people. Before a new doge took office, he was presented to the people with the words, "Here is your doge, if he is pleasing to you." This presentation gradually became a mere formality, although it continued to be greeted with cheers.

Communes

A striking feature of life in a large number of Italian cities was the **commune**, an institution that probably began in the eleventh century. A commune was a unified body that acted as the "voice" of the entire town. All the members of the commune were businessmen who swore an oath of loyalty to one another and to the city. They pledged to defend their rights, even against their lord. Members of the nobility and the clergy were usually not allowed to join the commune.

The Italian commune was imitated all over Europe. Numerous cities received **charters** of freedom from their lords, granting the right of self-government in return for an annual tax payment. In England, where communes were known as **boroughs**, King John granted London the right to elect its own sheriff in 1199 and the right to elect its own mayor in 1215.

A number of bishops and other churchmen preached strongly against the communes, which they believed were destroying the social order. Many other lords seemed glad to see their subjects forming communes. A city that was a free commune attracted a great deal of business; the more business prospered, the more tax money the lord received.

Most free cities in northwest Europe were governed by a mayor and a town council. These officials served for set terms (the mayor of London's term of office was one year). At the end of this time they might choose their own successors. Alternatively, the new mayor and councilmen might be elected by a group of leading citizens—for instance, the master craftsmen of the city.

Even within these free cities, the power to vote was only held by a handful of people, usually the commune's wealthiest men. Lower-class people and women had little say in the affairs of running the city.

The image on this manuscript depicts King Edward III presenting revisions to the Magna Carta during his rule in the mid-1300s.

The Magna Carta

The Magna Carta, which translates from Latin to "Great Charter," was an important document penned during the Middle Ages. The charter was born out of an uprising against England's King John, who was heavily taxing his barons to fund a disastrous war with France. If the barons refused to pay, they met with severe punishment and the king took control of their lands. Under this tyranny, the barons fought back, seizing London and forcing the king to sign the Magna Carta as a peace treaty in 1215. This charter limited the power of the king, stating that he must follow the laws of the land. In total, the document had sixty-three clauses. Over the following centuries, the Magna Carta was revised several times. Three clauses remain part of English law today, the most famous of which, translated to modern-day English, reads:

> No free man shall be seized or imprisoned, or stripped of his rights or possessions, or outlawed or exiled, or deprived of his standing in any other way, nor will we proceed with force against him, or send others to do so, except by the lawful judgement of his equals or by the law of the land. To no one will we sell, to no one deny or delay right or justice.

Many ideas such as this, set forth in the Magna Carta, are echoed in modern-day documents, including the US Declaration of Independence and the Universal Declaration of Human Rights.

Chapter Three

Walled Cities

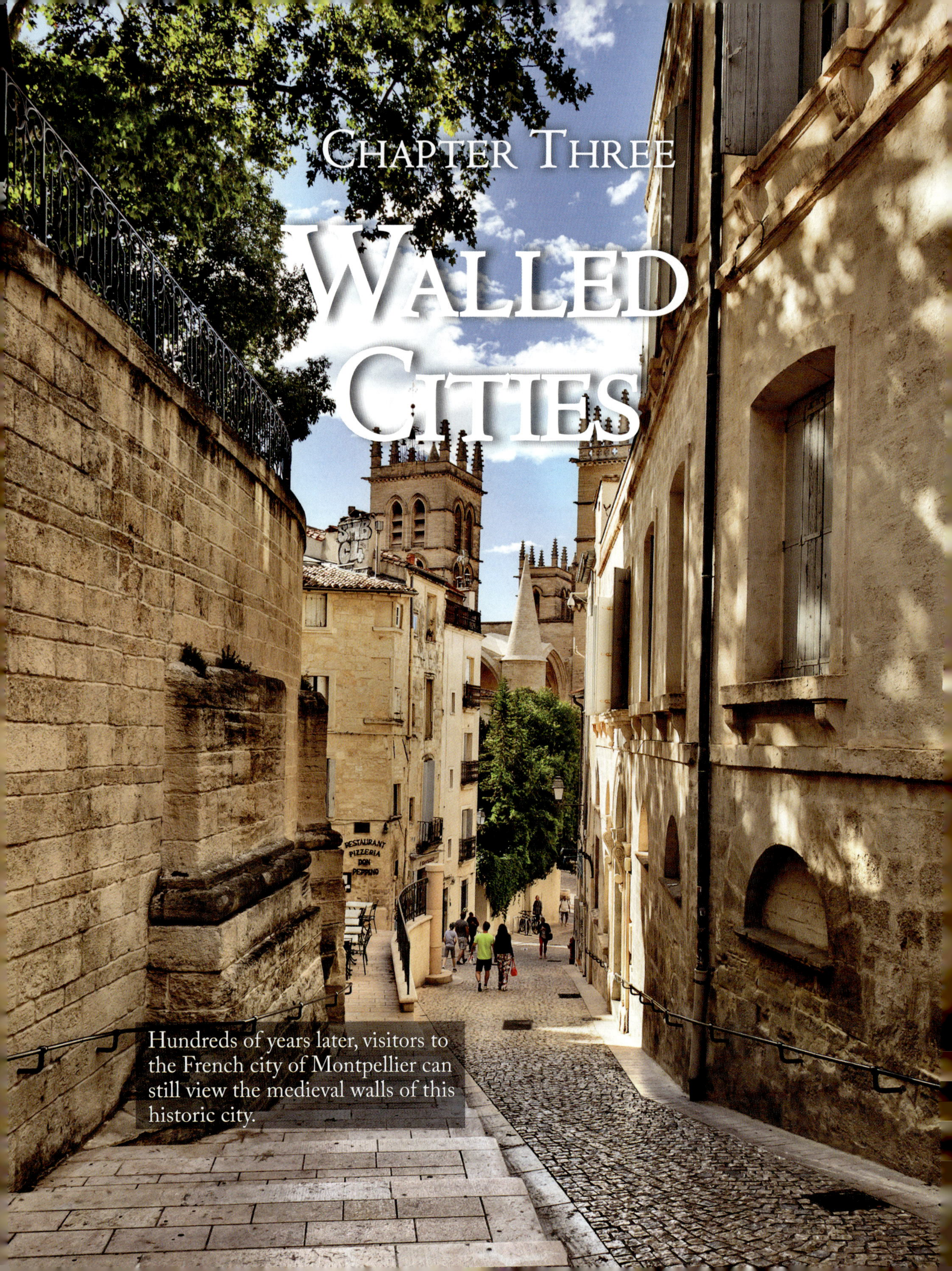

Hundreds of years later, visitors to the French city of Montpellier can still view the medieval walls of this historic city.

"Once inside the fortifications the visitor to Montpellier would have been confronted with a maze of narrow streets and crowded housing. Most of the private dwellings were of two stories … Open spaces—city squares, courtyards, or small orchards—would have provided some relief from the densely populated urban nucleus within the walls."

—a historian's description of life within the walls of medieval Montpellier

The Middle Ages were a violent period during which many cities came under attack. To guard against these attacks, protective stone walls were built around the city. As the city within swelled, the walls grew in size, and orchards and gardens were soon replaced with more buildings. Walled cities became cramped places to live; in the 1300s, the city of Montpellier, France, had a population density of about four hundred people per 1 acre (0.4 hectares). The Italian city of Venice did not need walls for protection; a powerful navy and waterways provided the city's defense.

A number of cities had not only walls but also a fortress or castle. In many cases, the castle had been there first, and the city had grown up around it. The city of Edinburgh, for example, took shape along the road that led between the king of Scotland's castle and Holyrood Abbey. (An abbey was a large monastery or **convent** headed by an abbot or abbess.) Sometimes a city without a castle decided that it needed greater protection from enemies and built a new fortress as an added defense. In 1202, the king of France ordered the building of a castle in Paris at a place by the Seine River where he thought the city's defenses were especially weak. The king himself did not live in the castle (he had a palace elsewhere in the city), but he did store his treasure there.

A Medieval Walking Tour

Visitors to a medieval city—perhaps attending a fair—entered through gates in the city's wall. They might have to cross a drawbridge over a moat first. Inside the wall they found streets lined with homes and businesses. Some buildings were painted red and blue or decorated in other ways. Signs with colorful pictures hung over the doorways of shops and taverns. Goods of all kinds were laid out on display on counters in front of the shops. Businesses of the same sort usually clustered together in the same part of the city or even on the same street. Visitors, as well as city residents, avoided the neighborhoods of the butchers and **tanners** (as much as possible—these trades produced extremely unpleasant smells).

Streets were crowded with pedestrians, horses, and carts. Cats, dogs, geese, chickens, pigs, sheep, and cattle were also likely to be in the street. Many cities had at least two main thoroughfares, often running east to west and north to south. These tended to be fairly wide and straight. Other streets, however, usually were not. Some Paris streets were so narrow that only one person at a time could walk down them. Most streets in medieval cities were unpaved, muddy, foul, and smelly. In 1185, the king of France could no longer stand the odor coming from the mud, and he gave orders for the main streets of Paris to be paved with stones.

Throughout the medieval city were open squares, often in front of churches and generally unpaved. Sometimes a group of houses was built around a small square. Usually a city had at least one square large enough to serve as a gathering place for much of the population. Ten thousand or more people at a time could assemble in the square in front of St. Mark's Basilica in Venice.

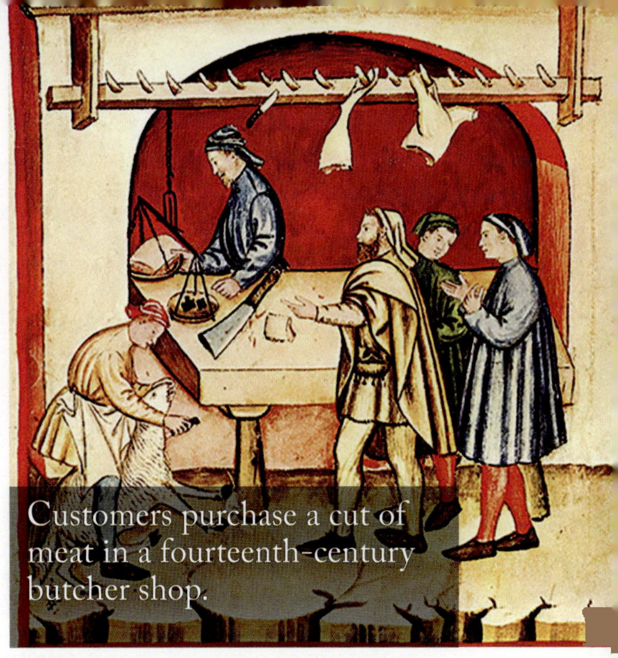

Customers purchase a cut of meat in a fourteenth-century butcher shop.

On the square in front of Notre Dame Cathedral in Paris, a pork market was held once a week. Most cities had various open-air markets, sometimes held in a church square and sometimes held in a district of the city dedicated to fairs and markets. Paris had a famous market called Les Halles, where the king had constructed two large buildings to shelter greengrocers, grain merchants, and dealers in small goods. Other towns also had permanent market buildings as well as open areas where visiting merchants could set up temporary stalls and tents.

Religious Centers

Every neighborhood had its own parish church. Medieval churches were not only places of worship but also social centers. Meetings of various kinds, including town councils, were often held in churches. There was a church service held every three hours, beginning at dawn. The ringing of the bells before each of these services marked the passage of time for city dwellers.

Many churches were dedicated to particular **saints**. The saints were people who had lived exceptionally holy lives and who had the power to perform miracles. Since God was often felt to be unreachable by ordinary humans, many Christians prayed to saints to "speak to" God on their behalf.

When seeking a saint's help, a person often prayed before a picture or statue of the saint or, if possible, at the saint's tomb or at a **shrine** to the saint.

Some shrines housed relics—physical remains (usually bones)—of the saint. Holy relics had a great reputation for miraculous powers. During the Middle Ages, people often traveled great distances on **pilgrimages** to visit churches that housed the relics of saints.

Some of the most splendid churches in medieval cities were the cathedrals. During the twelfth century, a new style of architecture became very popular and was used for many cathedrals (as well as other churches). This style later came to be known as Gothic architecture. Recently developed engineering techniques allowed stone structures to soar to lofty heights. This was very effective in the new cathedrals, where tall, pointed arches and other features naturally drew worshipers' eyes up toward heaven.

The new style of building also allowed large windows to be set into the high walls of the cathedrals. Since colored glass was actually easier to produce at this time than perfectly clear glass, the church designers made a virtue of necessity and created stained glass windows. At first, pieces of glass were joined together in lead frames to make abstract designs. Soon it was realized that pictures could be made with the colored glass. Stained glass windows illustrating episodes from the Bible and other religious scenes became an important feature of churches from then on. For many worshipers, who could neither read nor understand most of the church service (which was in Latin), these windows were their version of the Bible.

Probably the world's most famous Gothic cathedral is Notre Dame in Paris. Notre Dame, like many other Gothic cathedrals, took close to a century to complete. The work was done in stages, often halting for a time when money ran out. Yet no expense was spared in cathedral construction. Lords, prominent citizens, and groups of craftspeople all made donations to finance the new churches and their beautiful windows. These masterpieces in stone and glass not only glorified God but were also monuments to civic pride.

The World's First University

Students take notes during a lecture at the University of Bologna.

The world's oldest university was founded in 1088 in the medieval city of Bologna, Italy. Bologna was a student-run university; pupils paid their professors a *collectio*, which was considered a gift rather than a salary, to teach. Over time, however, these gifts turned into a regular salary. As the university grew, it became a center of study for civil and **canon law**. A professor describes his method for teaching law in 1250:

> First, I shall give you the summaries of each title before I come to the text. Second, I shall put forth well and distinctly and in the best terms I can the purport of each law. Third, I shall read the text [aloud] in order to correct it. Fourth, I shall briefly reinstate the meaning. Fifth, I shall solve conflicts, adding general matters (which are commonly called *broeadica*) and subtle and useful distinctions and questions with the solution, so far as Divine Providence shall assist me. And if any law is deserving of a review by reason of its fame or difficulty, I shall reserve it for an afternoon review session.

Around 1200, medicine and philosophy were studied at the school. The university grew in prestige and drew students from across Europe; during the thirteenth century there were over two thousand students in Bologna. During the 1400s, the university gained fame for performing human dissections. The university continues to operate today, nearly one thousand years later.

The Pursuit of Knowledge

In addition to their other functions, cathedrals were centers of learning. Most had a cathedral school, originally organized by the bishop to educate future priests. In the eleventh century, cathedral schools began to educate additional students, including sons of nobles, merchants, and other well-to-do citizens. By the twelfth century, there were many renowned cathedral schools in Europe. Each school tended to have its own specialty area of study, and students often traveled from school to school over the course of many years.

This was the beginning of the European university, a creation of the Middle Ages. By 1200, five great universities were taking form in the cities of Salerno and Bologna (Italy), Montpellier and Paris (France), and Oxford (England). By 1250, Europe boasted a total of twenty-two universities. Some were particularly noted for teaching law, others for medicine, and others for philosophy and religion.

University students might be as young as fourteen. For much of the Middle Ages, they did not live in dormitories or study in libraries; universities at this time had few, if any, permanent buildings. Instead classes were held in the homes of professors, or even in rooms over taverns. Students sat on the floor, listening to lectures and debating points of logic, all in Latin. At night they returned to rented rooms to read or copy **manuscripts** by candlelight. After six years or so of study, they might take an examination and receive a license to teach. They might also become churchmen, lawyers, or doctors, or enter the service of a king or noble.

With the growth of these urban learning centers, the quest for higher learning gradually became a vital element of city life across medieval Europe.

Connecting Communities

The eleventh century saw the beginning of a wave of bridge building in western Europe. Ferries were becoming inadequate to deal with the increasing number of medieval travelers, especially merchants with their carts and trains of packhorses. Local lords, who profited from tolls collected at river crossings on their lands, realized that bridges could be a source of needed cash. The Catholic Church recognized bridges as a great help to travelers, especially pilgrims, and supported their construction.

In the twelfth century, a group of devout men in southern France dedicated themselves to the good work of bridge building. These "Brothers of the Bridge" were responsible for the famous bridge of Avignon, which had a combination chapel and toll booth at one end. Even though the bridge became unusable in the 1600s, French children still sing and dance to an old folksong about it, "Sur le Pont d'Avignon" ("On the Bridge of Avignon").

Another medieval bridge later made famous in song was London Bridge. It was completed in 1209 and was the only bridge over the Thames River until 1750. Nineteen stone arches, each of them slightly different from the others, supported it. At one place in the bridge, there was a gap covered by a drawbridge. If the city was ever attacked, this drawbridge could be raised to prevent enemies from crossing. Drawbridges had long been used over castle moats, but this is the first known use of the drawbridge at a river crossing.

As with bridges in other medieval towns, there were many houses and shops on London Bridge. A bridge was a good place to live and work, because water could easily be drawn from the river. Medieval city dwellers dumped their trash and sewage into the rivers, so waste disposal was also more convenient for people who lived on bridges. Unfortunately, this added to the unhealthiness of city living conditions in general.

Chapter Four

Hearth and Home

Many medieval houses still stand in the German town of Schwäbisch Hall.

"Simon de Canterbury, carpenter, came before the Mayor and Aldermen on the Saturday next after the Feast of St. Martin the Bishop, in the second year of the reign of King Edward, son of King Edward, and acknowledged that he would make at his own proper charges, down to the locks, for William de Hanigtone, pelterer, before the Feast of Easter then next."

—an excerpt outlining the timeframe for a house to be built in London, England, dated November 16, 1308

Wood was the most common material used to build houses in medieval cities as it was the most affordable. Most wooden houses were narrow, stood up to four stories tall, and were covered with a thatched roof. As their wood frames aged, these houses started to lean. The upper levels often hung out over the narrow city streets, creating a canopy of sorts. Wealthier people were able to build their homes out of sturdier materials like brick or stone.

In poorer neighborhoods, several families lived in each house, renting their rooms from the house's owner. A very poor family might share only one room. This was often where they worked, as well as where they cooked, ate, slept, and so on. If the father or mother was a weaver by trade, the loom probably took up most of the family's quarters.

For most city people, their home was also their place of business. An independent craftsperson would have a shop and workshop on the ground floor of a house, and the family would live on the upper floors.

At the Kitchen Table

In medieval cities, most families purchased the bulk of their food from markets. This gave them greater access to a variety of foods from faraway lands, such as spices or wine. Bread was common on all medieval tables. Most breads were dark and dense as the wheat to make white bread was more expensive and could only be afforded by the wealthy. Thick stews, called pottages, were made by boiling grains and vegetables together for several hours over the fire. For those who could afford it, meat was also added. Fruits and vegetables were always cooked; it was believed that if they were eaten raw, they would make a person sick.

Wealthy merchants could have very large and splendid homes. In Venice, for example, such a house was usually three stories tall. The first level was given over to business. The front entrance, facing the water, had a quay or dock. (Venice had canals instead of streets, boats and ships instead of carts and trains of packhorses.) The central doorway led into a spacious hall where goods could be unloaded, counted, and inspected. On either side of this, and half its height, were storerooms. The merchant had his offices on an in-between level above the storerooms. On the second floor was a large central hall that was often used as a showroom for merchandise. It was also the place where banquets, weddings, and other gatherings were held. To the sides of this hall were the family's living quarters. The top floor provided rooms for servants and employees.

Inside the Home

Even for wealthy families, living conditions were not what we would think of as comfortable. Fireplaces were the only source of heat and often the main source of light. Oiled parchment was the most common window covering, and windows were usually small and narrow to begin with. Oil lamps and smoky tallow candles tended to be lit only after dark.

The main room of a private house, sometimes called the solar, was where the family dined. It contained benches, one or two cupboards for storing dishes and utensils, and a **trestle table** (which was only set up at mealtimes). In well-to-do homes, panels of dyed or embroidered cloth hung on the walls. Beginning in the early 1300s, tapestries—more elaborate wall hangings—became available to the wealthy. At this time, too, rugs began to be common in European cities; before this, floors were usually covered only with rushes, sometimes with fragrant herbs and flowers added.

Within the tight confines of a city's walls, green spaces were shared by many citizens as community gardens.

The kitchen was often behind the solar. The kitchen's main feature was a huge fireplace, where all the cooking was done. There was a long worktable, a large vat for water, and a spice cabinet. Of course the kitchen also contained pots, **cauldrons**, **trivets**, mortars and pestles, spoons, and a number of other cooking utensils. Many houses had small gardens to supply the kitchen with herbs and vegetables.

Bedroom furniture included a washstand, a chest, and perhaps a table and a few chairs. Adults slept in huge canopied beds; children's beds were smaller and plainer. There were no closets for clothes. Garments were stored in chests or hung up on hooks on the wall or on a rod behind the bed. People slept naked or in their underclothes.

Cleanliness was a challenge in the medieval city. Water for drinking, cooking, and washing had to be carried from a well outside the house. Many households often shared a single well. People generally bathed once a week at most. Fleas, bedbugs, and lice were constant problems. To go to the bathroom, most people had to use an outhouse in the yard. At night, they could use a chamber pot that was kept under the bed. Some homes might have a **garderobe**, a kind of indoor outhouse, off the bedroom. Garderobes often emptied into nearby canals, streams, or ditches, contributing to unsanitary conditions in medieval cities.

Despite the cramped and sometimes filthy living conditions, people continued to flock to the medieval city throughout much of the Middle Ages.

The spices and seasonings for many medieval recipes were purchased at an apothecary's shop.

A Feast of Flavor

In the Middle Ages, spices were a luxury. Merchants who traded in spices could make huge profits. These merchants and other well-to-do city dwellers enjoyed highly spiced food. From near Venice comes a recipe for a spice mixture that could be used "for all foods": one part black pepper, one part cinnamon, one part ginger, one-quarter part saffron, and one-eighth part cloves.

Another spicy medieval recipe, this time from England, is for a kind of ginger candy: Boil a quart of honey, and skim off any scum that rises to the top. Remove from heat and add a pinch of saffron, a pinch of white pepper, and a few pinches each of ginger and cinnamon. Thoroughly stir in plain, white breadcrumbs—enough to make the honey a very thick mass. Let the mixture cool slightly, then pour it out onto a flat surface and pat it into a square or rectangle. When it is cooled completely, cut it into small squares, stick a whole clove into each square, and enjoy!

Chapter Five

The City Community

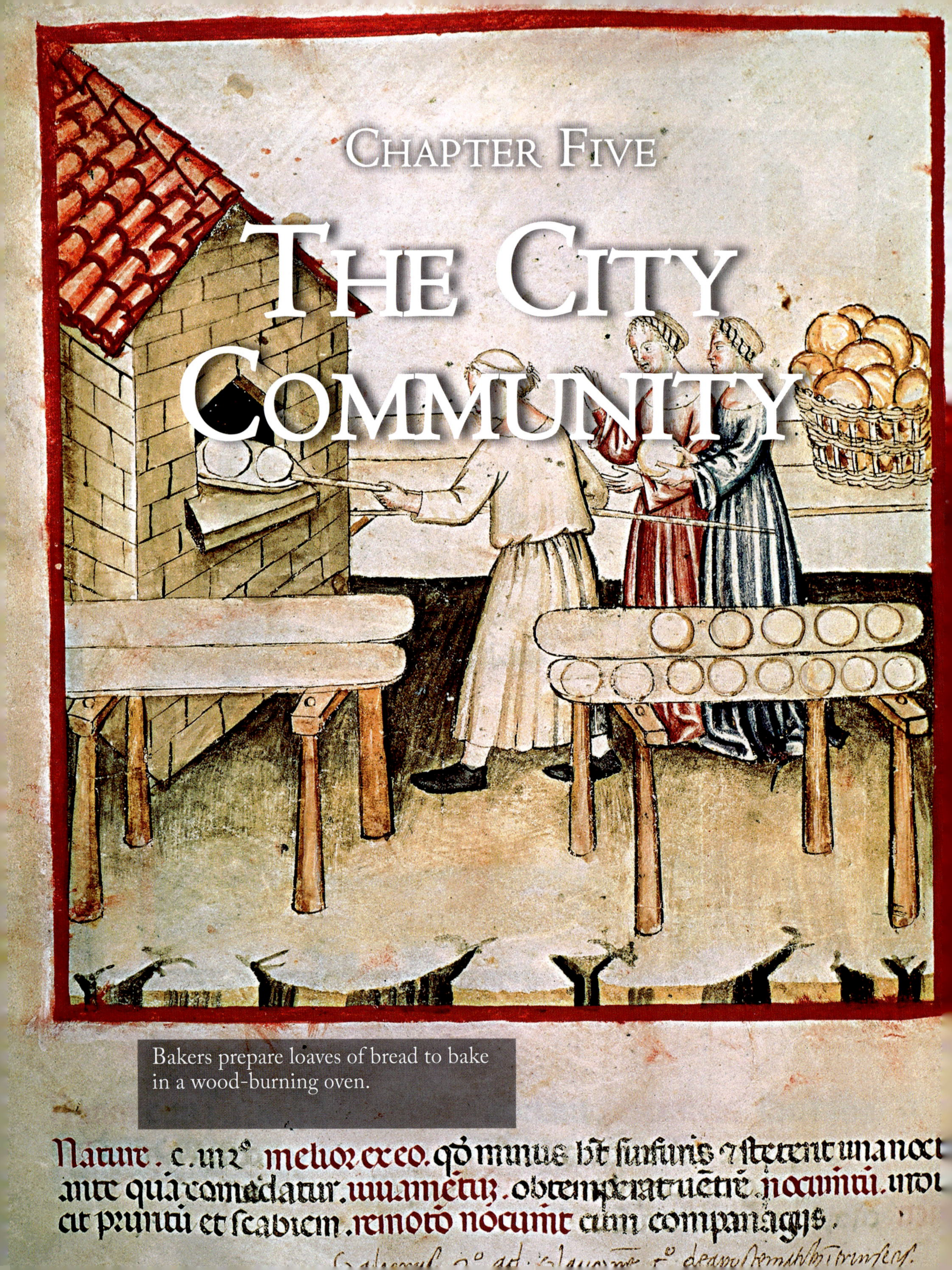

Bakers prepare loaves of bread to bake in a wood-burning oven.

"When a Quarter of Wheat is sold for 12d., then Wastel Bread of a farthing shall weigh £6 and 16s. But Bread Cocket of a farthing of the same grain and bultel, shall weigh more than Wastel by 2s. And Cocket Bread made of grain of lower price, shall weigh more than Wastel by 5s. Bread made into a Simnel shall weigh 2s. less than Wastel. Bread made of the whole Wheat shall weigh a Cocket and a half, so that a Cocket shall weigh more than a Wastel by 5s. Bread of Treet shall weigh 2 wastels. And bread of common wheat shall weigh two great cockets."

—regulations on the weight of bread from the the Assizes of Bread, Beer, & Lucrum Pistoris

During the early Middle Ages, society was largely made up of just two classes: the wealthy nobility, which included kings, lords, and the clergy; and the peasants, who worked the land. The rise of the city gave those from the lower class a chance to create their own wealth and gain independence that was not achievable under **manorialism**.

This new class of people—the middle class—became increasingly important in European society. These people were not rulers or nobles with large landholdings, and they were not peasant farmers or common laborers. They were a middle class: merchants, bankers, doctors, lawyers, and skilled craftspeople. Middle-class property owners and master craftsmen—called **bourgeois, burghers, burgesses**, or similar names in much of northwest Europe—were a town's leading citizens. They paid a share of the borough's annual tax to the king and enjoyed a number of privileges in return, including the rights to vote and hold city offices.

Although burghers were highly influential, their numbers were relatively small. Most city residents were common working people with no say in how the city was run. Many of these people lived comfortably enough, but others were very poor. Some were unable to make a regular living and resorted to begging. This became a greater problem as increasing numbers of peasants left the countryside in the hope of gaining freedom and finding more profitable work in the towns.

Hospitals began to appear in a number of medieval cities. These hospitals were usually established by the Catholic Church and run by monks and sometimes nuns. They not only treated sick people but also fed and clothed the poor. Some hospitals also provided food and shelter for pilgrims, and others cared for orphans. Saint Catherine's Hospital in Paris gave free lodging to poor widows and young girls who came to the city looking for work. By 1180, Paris also had three colleges, which provided cheap housing for impoverished university students.

From Far and Away

Medieval cities were meeting places for people of many nationalities. A city where the king held court would be visited from time to time by foreign ambassadors. If a city had a university, it attracted students from all over Europe. Pilgrims, too, journeyed to cities in a number of different countries. Other visitors or temporary residents in towns were traveling preachers and wandering entertainers.

Cities that were erecting new churches and cathedrals "imported" many of the skilled craftspeople needed for the construction. These workers, from a variety of places, often lived in temporary housing right in the cathedral yard. Master **masons**, master carpenters, bell **founders**, and window makers in

Getting from One Place to Another

A band of wealthy city dwellers travel together on horseback.

Many merchants and travelers followed the route of old Roman roads when traveling between one city and another. These roads tended to follow the natural contours of the landscape. Bridges were not common outside of major cities, although at some river crossings, a small fee could be paid for a boat to ferry a traveler across. Or, if the water was shallow enough, a brave person might cross by foot or on horseback.

Horseback was the most common way to travel, for those who could afford to buy or rent a horse. Travel times varied; a single rider could travel much faster than a horse pulling a cart loaded with goods to sell.

There were many dangers on the roads, such as roaming bands of thieves. Often many people would travel together for safety. A lord might also have security forces patrolling along roads running through their lands to protect travelers and promote trade. Additionally, if a merchant were robbed, some lords would compensate the traveler for the value of goods lost. A 1285 English law even ordered that brush be cut back 200 feet (61 meters) on either side of the road to provide fewer places for thieves to hide.

Many rivers became natural highways to transport people and goods. A boat moving downstream could travel about 80 miles (129 kilometers) in a single day. Travel by sea grew in popularity as ships and tools for navigation advanced. A trip between England and France lasted about four days, while a journey from Venice to Jaffa, the port of Jerusalem, took about one month.

particular traveled from building site to building site as their services were needed.

Trade was the force that brought the most visitors of all into the medieval city. The great fairs held twice a year in the French city of Troyes attracted merchants not only from across France but also from Spain, Italy, Germany, Flanders, England, Scotland, and Scandinavia. Venice had so many foreign merchants visiting on a regular basis that in the early 1300s the city began to construct permanent business centers. Venetian merchants themselves voyaged to most of the known world, everywhere from England to North Africa to Constantinople and beyond. Many Venetians and others lived and did business in foreign cities for years at a time.

Medieval cities commonly had large Jewish populations. Catholic Church law prohibited Jews from owning land and from earning their living by manufacturing or selling goods to the general public. At the same time, Christians were generally forbidden to make loans and charge interest. Jews were therefore able to play an important role as bankers and moneylenders in many cities.

City governments were often tolerant of Jews, especially when this proved profitable. All too often during the Middle Ages, however, a ruler needing money would expel the Jews from the area under his rule, confiscating all of their property and belongings. This happened in Paris in 1182. Sixteen years later, the banished Jews were allowed to return to the city, but only after paying a tax to the king.

Even worse, Jews were sometimes targets of extreme violence. For example, in 1190, 150 Jewish men, women, and children were killed in the city of York, England. Even in the international atmosphere of the medieval city, the Christian majority had difficulty understanding and accepting religious differences.

A World Traveler

A fifteenth-century manuscript shows Kublai Khan, in his royal court, presenting the Polo brothers with a golden tablet.

The most famous of all medieval merchants was Marco Polo. In 1271, at the age of seventeen, Marco Polo left Venice with his father and uncle. They were heading for China, which the two older men had already visited once. After a four-year journey, the Polos reached China's eastern coast and the court of the emperor, Kublai Khan.

The emperor was extremely impressed with Marco Polo's abilities and took the young Venetian into his service. Over the course of the next seventeen years, Marco was given numerous diplomatic missions, which took him not only all over China but also to India, Persia, Tibet, Burma (today's Myanmar), and Vietnam. Everywhere he went, he carefully observed and remembered scenery, people's customs, and details of local trade.

At last the Polos grew homesick, and in 1292 they set out for Venice. Arriving home after an arduous journey over land and sea, they were greeted with astonishment and disbelief. The tales they told of their travels and their long stay in the East were incredible. The rich robes and fabulous jewels they brought back, proof of the wealth of the East, made a deep impression on their fellow Venetians.

As for Marco, he eventually turned the story of his adventures into a book. *The Travels of Marco Polo* became a medieval best seller. Aside from describing the wonders of the East, Marco's book provided extremely accurate geographical information. For centuries, his book was referred to by mapmakers and explorers, including Christopher Columbus.

Marco Polo died in 1324. It is said that his last words were, "I did not write half of what I saw."

Chapter Six

A Center of Commerce

Today, artisans in Murano, near Venice, Italy, use many of the same techniques developed by glassblowers during the Middle Ages to craft beautiful works of art.

"If any of our burgesses should wish to practice the craft of weaving he ought to have one spindle or as many as two, and he should place them in his house, and for every spindle he should pay three solidi on entry into the fraternity. But if he should not pay the denarii within the said time and he afterwards cease to be of the craft he cannot regain it except with twenty-three solidi."

—a regulation from the Weavers' Gild of Stendal, 1233

Several medieval cities grew as centers of industry, becoming renowned for specialized items that brought them fame and fortune. Many of these items were luxurious and became highly sought by members of the noble class and wealthy city folk. From Flanders they desired woolen cloth; from Lucca, silk; from Venice, glass; and from Milan, armor and weaponry.

The citizens of a prosperous medieval town might work at more than a hundred different crafts and trades. In a large city like Paris, the number of different occupations could be close to two hundred. Many trades were family affairs, with husband, wife, and children all sharing in the work. Sometimes husband and wife worked at two different trades, however. Widows and single women often supported themselves (and sometimes their children, too) through crafts or various businesses.

A group of female weavers spinning and weaving cloth are shown in this fifteenth-century manuscript.

In much of Europe during the High Middle Ages, women worked at almost as many kinds of jobs as men did. We have records from around 1300 that tell of women—especially in France, Germany, and England—who were merchants, money changers, jewelers, goldsmiths, artists, stone masons, entertainers, tavern keepers, shoemakers, leather workers, shield makers, archers, gatekeepers, millers, blacksmiths, brewers, wine dealers, food sellers, fishmongers, bakers, peddlers, dyers, yarn makers, wool weavers, linen workers, tailors, dressmakers, hat makers, furriers, hairdressers, candle makers, spice dealers, pharmacists, doctors, surgeons, and barbers (who not only cut hair but also performed minor surgery and set broken bones). Only a few professions were totally closed to women at this time: they could not be sailors, notaries, lawyers, or priests. As household servants, laundresses, nurses, wax dealers, silk spinners, silk weavers, embroiderers, and lace makers, Parisian women outnumbered men in 1292. Unfortunately, as in so many other times and places, medieval women routinely earned less money than men, even for the same work.

Women who didn't work for pay still worked hard, raising children and keeping house. Even with a servant or two to help, household chores were time consuming and often demanded a great deal of strength from the medieval housewife. Only women in very wealthy families avoided physical labor completely.

A Fellowship of Trades

During the Middle Ages, people who worked at the same craft or trade typically belonged to a **guild**. Guilds set standards for products and workmanship, regulated wages and employment practices, paid for members' funerals, and looked after members' interests in other ways.

Murano Glass

Glassmaking brought immense wealth to the great city of Venice. In 1291, fearing the spread of fire in the crowded streets, the city banned furnaces and moved its glassmaking facilities less than a mile north to the island of Murano. This move also helped safeguard the prized secrets of master glassblowers. Anyone caught sharing these secrets might be punished with a prison sentence, or even put to death. Glassmakers were highly regarded in Venetian society and enjoyed several privileges, including the right to wear a sword, and their daughters could marry into noble families.

The glass was created using sand from local rivers and barilla, a soda ash, brought to Venice from Syria. Loads of wood arrived each day by boat to feed the large furnaces. Each furnace had three levels; the bottom, where a roaring fire was stoked to produce a high amount of heat; the middle, called the crucible, where glass was melted at about 2200 degrees Fahrenheit (1200 degrees Celsius); and the top, where the glass cooled at lower temperatures. To fashion glass objects, a hollow blowing rod, made out of iron, was used to pick up a hot ball of glass from the crucible. Glassmakers would then gently blow into the rod and use tongs to shape the glass into mirrors, goblets, beads, and other luxurious items. To color the glass, metallic oxides were added. Cobalt was added to create blue glass, copper for red and gold, manganese for purple, and chromium for green.

A young apprentice is instructed by a master goldsmith in the craft of shaping the precious metal.

Around 1300, Paris had five guilds whose members were all women; Cologne (Germany) had four. In both cities, these women-only guilds were primarily dedicated to various stages in the making of silk cloth. There were many guilds in a number of cities where women were very active in their own right, even though most members were male. In other guilds, women could not be admitted unless they were wives, widows, or, sometimes, daughters of male guild members. It seems that virtually the only guilds that were completely closed to women throughout Europe were the guilds of the great merchants.

One of the guild's most important functions was to regulate the training of **apprentices**, or student craftspeople. Depending on the difficulty of the craft, an apprentice spent from four to twelve years learning his or her trade from a master. During this time, the apprentice usually lived in the master's home, and the master supplied the apprentice with food and clothing as well as training. The apprentice not only learned from but also assisted the master, even helping out with household chores when necessary.

When apprentices finished their training, they had to demonstrate to the guild that they knew their craft or trade, and they had to show that they had the money or tools to go into business for themselves. They swore that they were loyal and careful and that they would practice their profession honestly and responsibly. Finally, after paying a fee, they were accepted as masters and full members of their guild.

A Hard Day's Labor

Not all workers in medieval cities belonged to guilds. Some trades did not have guilds. Some people worked at their craft, even training apprentices, without ever belonging to the guild for it. However, most city dwellers did not have specialized, skilled crafts or trades. Unskilled laborers probably made up the majority of workers in the medieval city. Often they had no regular employment, but took whatever jobs were available each day. In addition, many townspeople were involved in agriculture. Every morning they left the city to work in fields, orchards, vineyards, or pastures outside the city walls. They returned to their urban homes and the safety of the city's walls before watchmen or guards closed the city gates for the night.

The workday for most people was long, lasting between ten and fourteen hours. On Sundays, much to the disdain of the Catholic Church, many people preferred to rest rather than attend church services.

Chapter Seven

An Urban Upbringing

The children of wealthy city families were often cared for by both their mothers and hired nurses.

"How many miles to Beverleyham?
Eight, eight, and other eight.
May I come there by daylight?
Yes, by God, if your horse be light."
—a thirteenth-century children's rhyming game

During the medieval period, babies were not born in hospitals. Instead, a midwife would come to a woman's home to deliver her baby. However, even with the assistance of a midwife, many mothers and their babies did not survive childbirth.

During labor, a city woman was often visited and encouraged by various female relatives, friends, and neighbors. No men were allowed to be present. In a well-to-do household, dishes of candied fruits and nuts were put out for the benefit of these visitors, and some of the family's best possessions were displayed in the birthing room.

Even in wealthy families, childbirth was difficult and dangerous. No one at this time knew about the risk of infection or about ways to prevent it. If something went wrong while a woman was giving birth, there was little the midwife could do. Sometimes she would whisper magical chants into the mother's ears, even though the Catholic Church disapproved of such things. Many babies and mothers died during or soon after birth.

If everything went well, the midwife immediately washed the newborn baby and then wrapped it securely in swaddling bands. These bands were tight enough to keep the baby from moving, for fear that too much movement would cause its arms and legs to twist out of shape. Then the baby was shown to its father for the first time.

Soon afterward, in a Christian family, the baby was taken to church to be baptized. A female relative carried the child, followed by the father, the godparents, the midwife, and various friends and family members; the mother, however, remained at home. During the ceremony, a priest anointed the baby with oil and dipped him or her into holy water. The godparents assisted, giving their promise to see that the child was raised according to the teachings of the Catholic Church. Townspeople often liked to choose rich and important citizens to be their children's godparents.

Back at home, the newborn was placed in a wooden cradle at its mother's bedside. Nearly all medieval babies were breast-fed, but well-to-do city dwellers generally hired a servant, called a nurse, for this purpose. The nurse fed and bathed the baby every three hours.

Early Years

When babies were old enough to sit up, they were released from their swaddling. From then on they wore clothes that were similar to what adults wore. About half of all children died before they reached the age of five. Those who lived spent their early years mostly playing. Children in well-off families might have tops, wooden swords, hobby horses, stilts, marbles, dolls made out of wood or clay, and similar toys. Other children had to use their imaginations and whatever they could find—sticks, leaves, flowers, horseshoes, blocks of wood, and even bread crusts. Many children had fun with balloons made

Games like chess and checkers were popular pastimes for people of all ages.

A Mother's Lullaby

From the Sloane manuscript, dating from the fifteenth century, the medieval lullaby "Lullay, mine liking" describes the birth of Jesus Christ from the Christian faith. A modern English translation reads:

I saw a fair maiden sit and sing,
She lulled a little child, a sweet lording:
Lullay, mine Liking, my dear Son, mine Sweeting,
Lullay, my dear Heart, mine own dear Darling.
That very lord is He that made all things
Of all lords He is Lord [and] King of all kings.
Lullay, mine Liking, my dear Son, mine Sweeting,
Lullay, my dear Heart, mine own dear Darling.
There was mickle [much] melody at that Childës birth,
All that were in heaven's bliss, they made mickle mirth.
Lullay, mine Liking, my dear Son, mine Sweeting,
Lullay, my dear Heart, mine own dear Darling.
Angels bright they sang that night and saiden to that Child,
"Blessed be Thou, and so be she that is both meek and mild."
Lullay, mine Liking, my dear Son, mine Sweeting,
Lullay, my dear Heart, mine own dear Darling.
Pray we now to that Child, and to His mother dear,
Grant them His blessing that now maken cheer.
Lullay, mine Liking, my dear Son, mine Sweeting,
Lullay, my dear Heart, mine own dear Darling.

This medieval artwork shows the Virgin Mary holding Jesus Christ as an infant.

from the bladders of recently slaughtered pigs. Like adults, children might enjoy games such as chess, checkers, backgammon, dice games, lawn bowling, wrestling, and blindman's bluff.

Around the age of seven, children began to prepare for their adult roles. Some boys and girls in medieval cities attended grammar school, where they learned basic arithmetic and reading. Boys could go on to more advanced studies at a cathedral school, and then perhaps at a university. For girls, the rest of their education usually took place at home and focused on cooking, cloth making, and other skills needed to run a household and care for a family. However, a number of girls as well as boys began an apprenticeship sometime between the ages of seven and twelve. Many others went straight to work, doing whatever was necessary to assist their parents.

Girls often married as teenagers, with fourteen being the age when a young woman could legally marry. Soon afterward, most became mothers themselves. Ten or fifteen years later, they might well find themselves widows, as during the Middle Ages it was common for young girls to marry men who were often ten, twenty, or thirty years their senior. Boys often married a few years later, once they had learned a trade and were able to provide for a family of their own.

Hunt the Slipper: A Medieval Game

This game was enjoyed by both children and adults in medieval towns and cities, where cobbling (repairing shoes) was a common trade.

To play hunt the slipper, the players need to sit in a tight circle on the floor or in chairs. One player, called Slipper Soul, sits or stands in the middle of the circle. She or he should be holding a slipper or shoe. While the other players pretend to be cobblers hard at work, Slipper Soul says:

Cobbler, cobbler,
Mend my shoe!
Make it all anew.
Three stitches will do!

With that, Slipper Soul hands the shoe or slipper to one of the players in the circle, then closes his or her eyes for several seconds. The other players pass the shoe from one to another behind their backs. When Slipper Soul's eyes are open again, everyone continues to pretend that they are passing the shoe around the circle. Slipper Soul must guess who actually has it. When that person is identified, he or she takes the shoe into the middle of the circle, becoming the next Slipper Soul, and the game begins all over again!

Chapter Eight

Food and Festivities

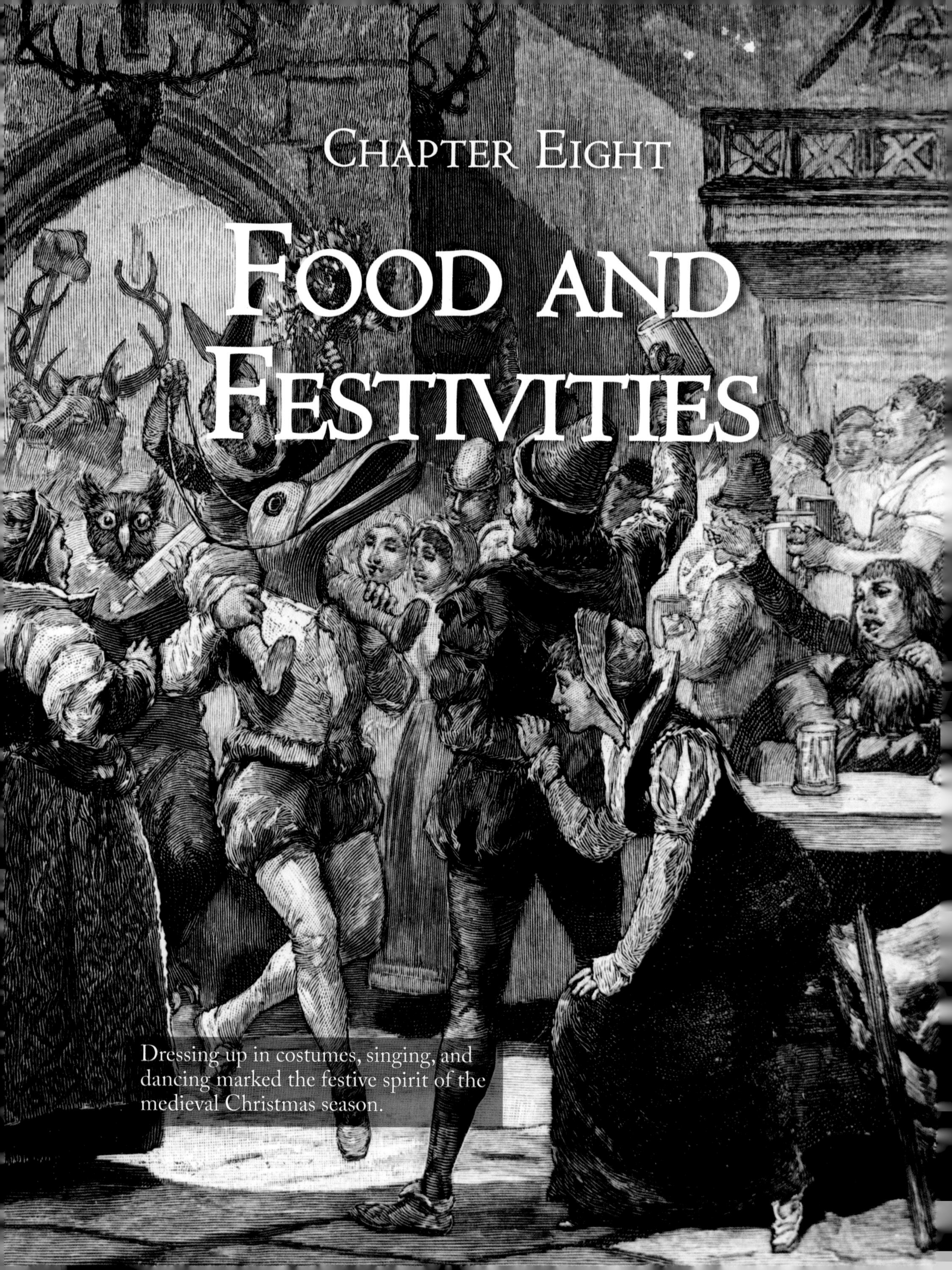

Dressing up in costumes, singing, and dancing marked the festive spirit of the medieval Christmas season.

"The boar's head in hand bear I,
Bedecked with bays and rosemary;
And I pray you, my masters, be merry,
Quo testis in convicio. [So many as are in the feast.]
Caput apri defero, [The boar's head I bring.]
Reddens laudes Domino. [Giving praises to God.]"
—a verse from "The Boar's Head Carol"

Many celebrations marked the medieval calendar, during which work stopped and a city's citizens were able to rest and take part in celebrations and feasting.

Most of these holidays were Christian feast days, although oftentimes the celebrations were loud and boisterous rather than reverent. Venice celebrated the Feast of the Purification of the Virgin Mary (February 2) with boat races on the city's Grand Canal. On the Feast of the Holy Innocents (December 28), French choirboys switched places with cathedral officials and conducted the church services. Another holiday saw low-ranking priests wearing their robes inside out, nibbling sausages in church, and braying like donkeys during the worship service!

As with Christians today, the most important medieval holidays were Christmas and Easter. Before each, there was a period of many weeks when people were supposed to turn their thoughts away from worldly pleasures,

A Yuletide Feast

The Christmas season lasted for twelve days, from December 25 to January 6. With the harvest finished, this was a time for sumptuous dining and merriment. In noble homes, an elaborately decorated roast goose or swan might be served. Boar's head was also a popular choice for holiday feasts. A Christmas pudding, called frumenty, was prepared from porridge, egg yolks, currants, and other fruits and served alongside venison. In the thirteenth century, the bishop of Hereford invited forty-one guests to an elaborate Christmas feast. He served boar's head, beef, pork, partridge, geese, bread, and cheese. He also supplied his guests with 40 gallons (151 liters) of red wine, and another 4 gallons (15 L) of white.

spend extra time in prayer, and purify themselves of sin as much as possible. When Christmas and Easter finally arrived, everyone celebrated as lavishly as they could afford to. Wealthy families had elaborate feasts, serving up to ten courses. Such feasts often included entertainment by musicians, singers, jugglers, and acrobats.

Plays were another favorite holiday entertainment in medieval cities. In the church services for Christmas and Easter, priests often acted out parts of the Bible stories of Jesus's birth and resurrection. These mini-plays were all in Latin, but they were so popular with worshipers that longer plays were eventually presented in French, German, and English. By the thirteenth century, Christmas and Easter plays were being given outdoors in front of the church. The plays portrayed episodes from the Bible, such as the story of Adam and Eve, as well as stories of the lives and miracles of various saints. Comedy was combined with serious religious lessons so that the watchers would stay interested.

In a Corpus Christi play, a scene from Jesus's last days is staged in a city square. These performances included all-male casts, as women were not allowed to act.

A number of English towns gradually developed cycles of plays that dramatized all the major events in the Bible, from the Creation to the Last Judgment. These play cycles came to be presented in squares and marketplaces around the feast of Corpus Christi (fifty-four days after Easter), which was celebrated with splendid processions through the city streets. Each individual play was produced by a specific guild, with guild members acting all the parts. In these English towns and in other medieval European cities, theater was evolving into the art form we know today.

On Pilgrimage to Canterbury

Geoffrey Chaucer, a resident of London, was one of the greatest writers in English literature. He was born around 1340 and died in 1400. His most famous book is *The Canterbury Tales*, in which a group of people on a pilgrimage to the Shrine of Saint Thomas à Becket in Canterbury entertain one another by telling stories. Several of the pilgrims are typical city dwellers; among them are the Merchant, the **Clerk**, the Five Guildsmen, and the Wife of Bath. Here, adapted into modern English, are Chaucer's descriptions of these urban travelers:

The Merchant

A merchant was there with a forked beard;
Richly clothed, high on his horse he sat.
On his head was an imported beaver-fur hat.
His boots were buckled most carefully.
He spoke his views very solemnly,
Always looking to the increase of his earnings.
He wished the sea kept safe more than anything.
. . .
This worthy man could use his head,
And no one knew if he was in debt,
So discreetly did he do his business,
With bargains and with making loans.

The Clerk

A clerk from Oxford was there also,
Who began to study logic long ago.
His horse was just as thin as a rake;

And he was not right fat, I undertake,
But looked hollow and full of care.
His outer cloak was all threadbare.
. . .
He would rather have by the head of his bed
Twenty books, bound in black or red,
Of Aristotle and his philosophy,
Than rich robes or music to make merry.
For all that he was a philosopher,
He had very little gold in his coffer;
But all he received that his friends lent,
On books and on learning it was spent,
And he would pray for the souls' ease
Of those who gave to him for his studies.
In thinking he took most care and most heed.
He spoke not one word more than he'd need,
And that was said in proper form and reverence,
And short and sweet, full of deep significance.
Full of moral virtue was his speech;
And gladly would he learn, and gladly teach.

The Five Guildsmen

A **haberdasher** and a carpenter,
A weaver, a dyer, and a rug maker—
They all wore the badge and garb bestowed
On members of a tradesmen's brotherhood.
. . .

Each of them seemed a fair burgess
To sit in a guildhall on the dais.
Every one, on account of his wisdom,
Was well suited to be a councilman.
As for property and income, they had plenty—
And with this their wives would well agree,
Or else they were certain to complain;
It is very pleasant to be called "Madame,"
To walk at the head of holy-day processions,
And to wear a cloak as fine as a queen's!

The Five Guildsmen on pilgrimage to Canterbury.

The Wife of Bath

From a suburb of Bath a good wife came,
But she was somewhat deaf, and that was a shame.
For making cloth she had such a bent,
She surpassed the famous weavers of Ghent.
. . .
Her many kerchiefs were finely textured—
I daresay that when she went to church,
They weighed ten pounds upon her head!
Her hose were of fine scarlet red,
Tightly tied, and her shoes were soft and new.
Bold was her face, and fair, and red of hue.
She was a worthy woman all her life.
As for husbands, she'd had five.
. . .
Three times she'd been to Jerusalem.
She had passed many a strange stream—
She had been to Rome and to Bologne,
To Saint James's shrine and to Cologne.
. . .
On an ambling horse she easily sat,
Bundled up well, on her head a hat
As wide around as a knight's shield,
A warm outer skirt from her hips to her heels.
On her feet she wore a pair of sharp spurs.
She laughed and joked with all the travelers.

Chapter Nine

Deadly Disasters

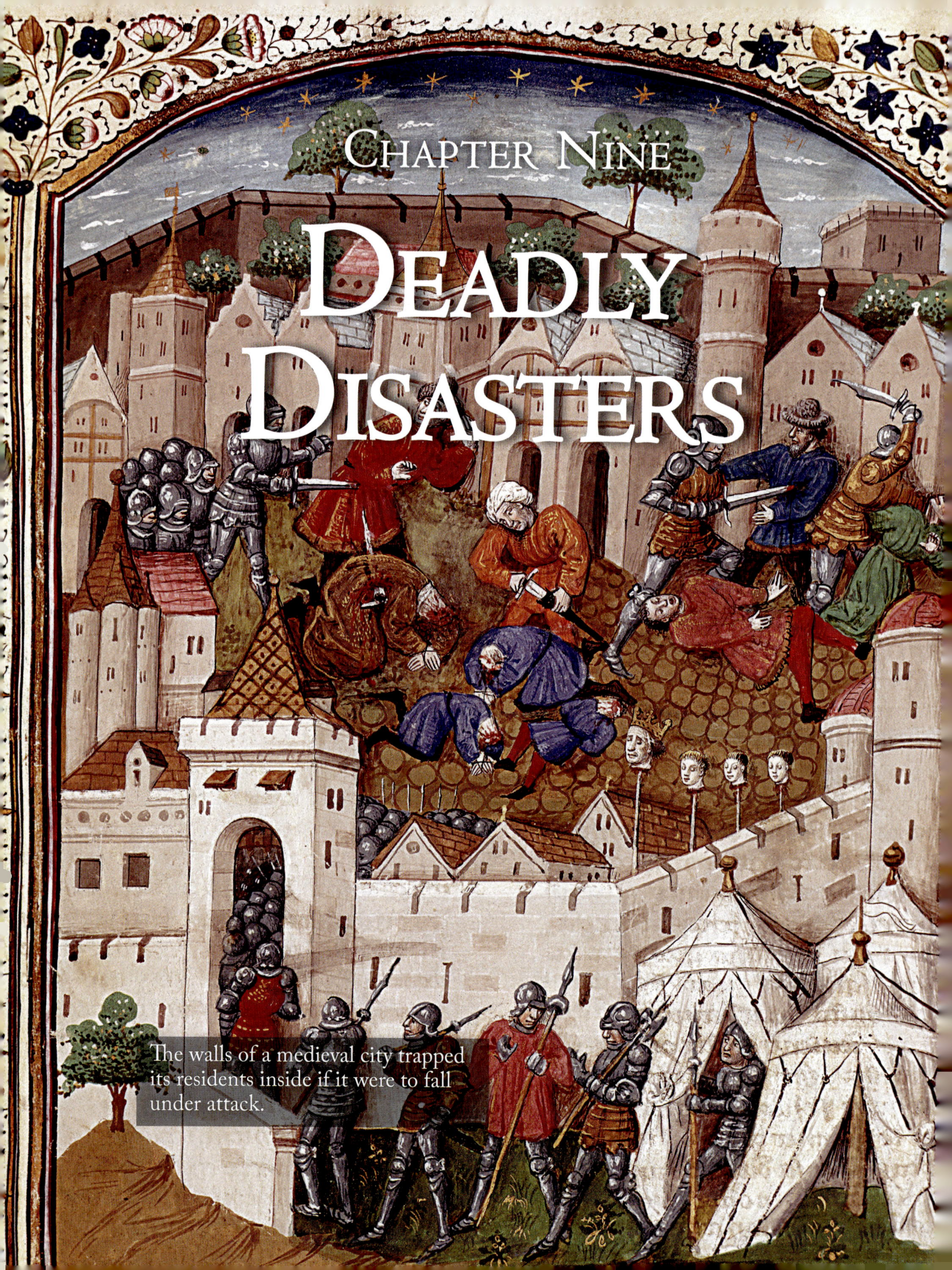

The walls of a medieval city trapped its residents inside if it were to fall under attack.

"So, in the year 1216, the Count entered the Cité with a large armed force. He started fires in several places hoping that the citizens would be put in dread by a double storm, of fire and sword, and thus be more readily thrown into confusion ... All night long they had no rest from fighting fire or the enemy."

—The Siege of Toulouse in 1217–1218, according to *The Chronicle of William of Puylaurens*

For most medieval cities, there were many dangers threatening the safety of the city as a whole. While strong walls provided a formidable defense against attacks, they also created a closed space in which fire and disease could rapidly spread, trapping the city's people inside.

Flooding was another threat as most medieval towns were built next to rivers or the sea. In 1197, a terrible flood struck Paris, swamping the bridges and wiping out whole neighborhoods. The city suffered almost equally bad floods in 1206, 1220, and 1221. Towns in the Netherlands were flooded repeatedly; one thirteenth-century flood killed more than fifty thousand people living near the Dutch coast.

Fire was a huge danger in all medieval cities; most urban buildings were built of wood and were crowded together. It took only one tipped-over candle or one spark from a fireplace to start a blaze that could destroy an entire

Flames destroyed homes on London Bridge, seen in the distance, in several fires throughout the Middle Ages and the centuries that followed.

neighborhood. When fire broke out, there were no professional firefighters to call on. Hastily organized bucket brigades were usually not enough to combat spreading flames.

Another constant threat was warfare. Italian city-states were frequently at war with one another. Other cities suffered in the conflicts between nations, such as the Hundred Years' War between England and France. City walls were usually strong enough to resist attackers—unless the attackers were able to tunnel under the wall. However, if an enemy laid siege to the city, the residents did not have enough food to hold out indefinitely. Even in times of peace, it could be difficult to ensure a constant food supply for medieval towns. Where there was war and hunger, diseases always followed.

The Plague

The worst disease of the Middle Ages was the Black Death. This fearful plague swept through western Europe repeatedly during the fourteenth through the seventeenth centuries. The first wave of the disease, from 1347 to 1350, was

The Great Fire of Southwark

In 1212, the city of London went up in flames with the Great Fire of Southwark. Written accounts document the fire starting south of the London Bridge, in Southwark. The flames quickly devoured the St. Mary Overie Cathedral, then traveled to the bridge, which caught fire. Many spectators rushed onto the bridge, both to watch the fire and to try to extinguish the flames. However, the wind blew and scattered the flames, igniting the far side of the bridge and trapping the doomed people between the two fires. It is believed three thousand people perished as a result of both the fire's flames and drowning in the river, while trying to escape.

the most devastating. Nearly every European city lost from one quarter to two thirds of its population. One chronicler recorded that between May and September of 1348, ninety-six thousand people died in Florence alone. Whole families were wiped out. There was no cure, and almost everyone who came down with the Plague died from it, usually within four days.

Many city dwellers fled to the countryside, hoping to escape the dreaded disease. There was no escape; the Black Death struck rural villages and country mansions, too. By the time the epidemic ended, western Europe had lost roughly half its population.

Christian Europeans tried to understand why God had allowed such a terrible disease to suddenly kill so many. Sometimes they blamed foreigners or other "strangers" for bringing the Plague to their city or country. The result was increased suspicion—and often persecution—of outsiders such as Jews and lepers (people who were already outcasts because they suffered from leprosy, a very serious skin disease).

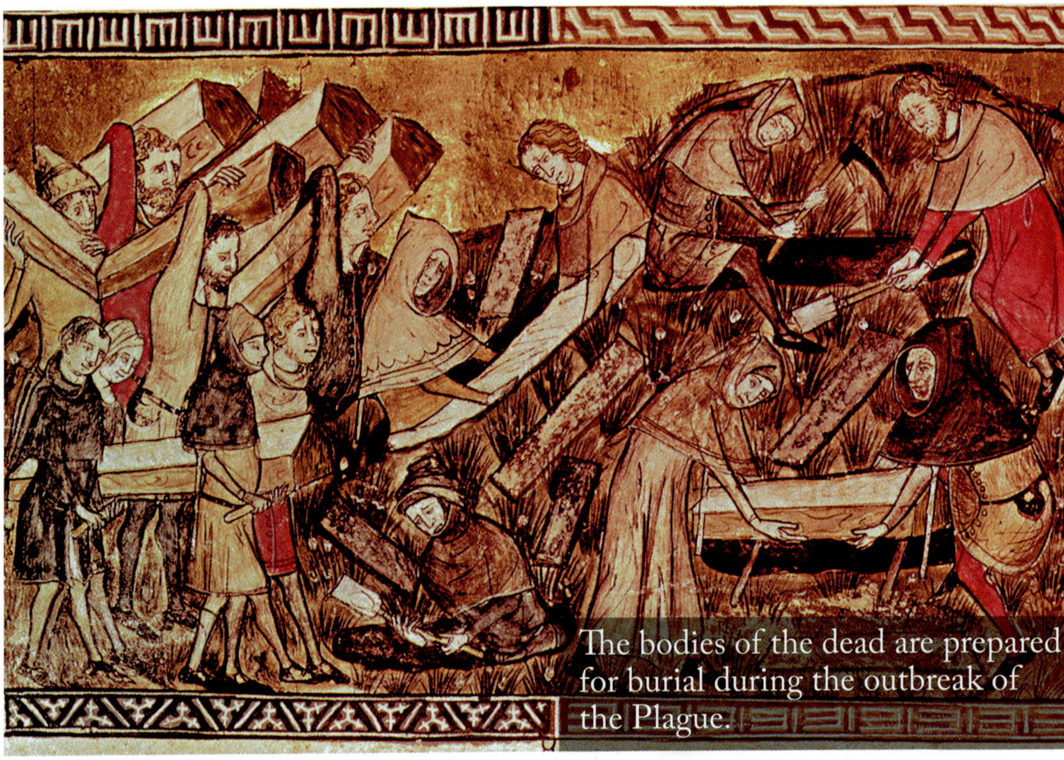

The bodies of the dead are prepared for burial during the outbreak of the Plague.

The Plague had other far-ranging effects on European society. Business and trade ground to a complete halt during the epidemic. When it was over, the economy had to be totally rebuilt. Labor was scarce and prices were high. Peasants and laborers demanded more rights and higher wages. Because of the scarcity and cost of labor, the Catholic Church permitted Christians to own non-Christian slaves. Governments passed laws that preserved the privileges of the upper class. Guilds tightened their rules, seeking to protect their members from competition, especially competition from women and others who would work for low wages.

After 1350, guilds and governments placed increasing limits on the work that women could do. For example, women were banned from being doctors on the grounds that they could not receive a university medical license. (They were not allowed to attend universities at all.) Some women continued to work as doctors—often with great success—but they were frequently arrested, tried, and fined for practicing medicine without a license. Women were banned from many crafts, too, and were admitted to fewer and fewer guilds. Not until the twentieth century would large numbers of women again enjoy the opportunity to work at the great variety of trades they had enjoyed in the city of the High Middle Ages.

Europe's towns did make some strides forward following the Black Death of 1347–1350. Public health became a new area of government concern as cities explored various measures to keep diseases from spreading. City governments, at least in northern Italy, had long been concerned with controlling pollution. Their efforts in this area increased, and there were efforts to improve sanitation as well.

Some cities were unable to survive the devastating effects of disease and disasters. Many others, however, carried on as rich centers of learning, culture, and trade. As travel across the Atlantic Ocean began during the Age of Exploration, many cities in North America were constructed based on traditions rooted in the bustling medieval cities of Europe.

Glossary

apprentice

An individual who works under another to learn a trade.

bishop

A high-ranking Catholic priest who oversees religious affairs for a particular region.

borough

English term for a town to which the king has granted the right of self-government, usually in return for an annual tax payment.

bourgeois

French name for a middle-class city dweller.

burgesses, burghers

English names for city dwellers, especially those who own property in a borough, pay part of the borough's annual tax to the king, and enjoy special privileges and full political rights in the borough.

canon law

The laws set out by a particular religion.

cathedral

A church from which a bishop presides.

cauldron

A large kettle.

charter

A document issued by a government or ruler that gives rights and power to a single person or group.

clerk

A priest or, as in *The Canterbury Tales,* a scholar studying for the priesthood.

commune

A group of leading citizens bound together by oath to run their businesses and govern their city without interference from an overlord; in general, a self-governing city.

convent

A group of women, called nuns, who live together and devote themselves to prayer and work; also, the building where the nuns live.

founder

A craftsperson who makes metal objects by melting metal and pouring it into molds.

garderobe

An alcove with a kind of toilet seat built over a chute or drainpipe that led to a pit in the house's cellar or to a nearby canal, stream, or ditch.

guild

An organization of people in the same craft or trade. The guild set standards of training and workmanship and looked after its members' interests in various ways.

haberdasher

A merchant dealing in small goods.

humanist

Someone adhering to a belief system based on a basic belief in goodness in people and that problems can be solved through rational reasoning, as opposed to religious faith.

Islam

The religion established in the Middle East by Muhammad in the early seventh century; the Islamic name for God is Allah, and Muhammad is revered as his prophet; followers of Islam are called Muslims.

manorialism

The arrangement between peasants and their lords, in which peasants held land from the lord and owed him various fees and services in exchange.

manuscript

A book that is written out, illustrated, and bound by hand.

mason

A skilled worker who cut stone into the right shapes for building or actually constructed the stone walls of a building.

monastery

A community of men who devote themselves to prayer, study, and work; also, the buildings that house such a community.

pilgrimage

A journey to an important religious site; for example, a church that houses the remains of a saint.

saint

A person recognized by the Catholic Church as being especially holy and able to perform miracles both in life and after death.

serf

An unfree peasant, with specific financial and labor obligations to an overlord

shrine

A place where people pray to one particular saint or other religious figure.

tanner

A person who boils animal skins to make leather.

trestle table

A table made by laying a large board across two or more supports

trivet

A metal stand placed under a hot dish at the table.

vassal

A noble who holds land from a king or more powerful noble in exchange for military service and a pledge of loyalty.

Further Information

Books

Baldwin, John. *Paris, 1200*. Palo Alto, CA: Stanford University Press, 2010.

Elliot, Lynne. *Medieval Towns, Trade, and Travel*. Medieval World. New York: Crabtree Publishing, 2004.

Frugoni, Chiara, and Arsenio Frugoni. *A Day in a Medieval City*. Translated by William McCuaig. Chicago: University of Chicago Press, 2005.

Hunt, Janin. *The University in Medieval Life*. Jefferson, NC: McFarland, 2008.

Jeffrey, Gary. *The Black Death*. Graphic Medieval History. New York: Crabtree Publishing, 2014.

Mount, Toni. *Everyday Life in Medieval London: From the Anglo-Saxons to the Tudors*. Gloucestershire, UK: Amberley Publishing, 2015.

Pirenne, Henri, and Michael McCormick. *Medieval Cities: Their Origins and the Revival of Trade*. Princeton, NJ: Princeton University Press, 2014.

Singman, Jerry L. *The Middle Ages: Everyday Life in Medieval Europe*. New York: Sterling, 2013.

Websites

BBC: The Black Death
www.bbc.co.uk/history/british/middle_ages/black_01.shtml
The BBC provides a comprehensive overview of the Plague and its spread throughout medieval Europe. The site includes primary source accounts from people who lived during this deadly period.

Museum of the City: Life and Times of Medieval Walled Cities
www.museumofthecity.org/project/the-life-and-times-of-medieval-walled-cities
Read all about the growth and significance of walled medieval cities.

Study.com: The Reemergence of Towns and Commerce
study.com/academy/lesson/the-reemergence-of-towns-and-commerce.html
Watch a video from Study.com on the resurgence of trade and the growth of cities during the Middle Ages.

Films

Going Medieval. The History Channel, 2013.

Scourge of the Black Death. The History Channel, 2005.

Organizations

Canadian Society of Medievalists
www.canadianmedievalists.ca/index.php?lang=en
The Canadian Society of Medievalists is an organization dedicated to medieval studies. The society publishes an annual journal, *Florilegium,* and hosts an annual conference for medieval enthusiasts.

The Medieval Academy of America
www.medievalacademy.org
As the largest medieval organization in the United States, the Medieval Academy of America focuses on all areas of life during the Middle Ages. The academy holds annual conferences, publishes research, and offers a student membership.

Source Notes

Chapter 1: The Rise of the Medieval City

p. 7, H. de Vere Stacpoole, Trans. *The Poems of Francois Villon.* New York: Press of J. J. Little and Ives Co, 1914, p 4–5, retrieved from https://archive.org/stream/poemsoffranoisrs00villuoft#pa.ge/n11/mode/2up

p. 11, Gies, Frances, and Joseph Gies. *Life in a Medieval City.* New York: Harper Perennial, 1969.

Chapter 2: Governing a City

p. 13, Excerpt from *Policraticus: Of the Frivolities of Courtiers and Footprints of Philosophers.* Kelley, Donald R., and Bonnie G. Smith, eds. *The Medieval & Early Modern World: Primary Sources and Reference Volume.* New York, Oxford University Press, 2005, p. 30.

p. 14–17, Hinds, Kathryn. *Venice and Its Merchant Empire.* Unpublished manuscript, 1997.

p. 19, "Magna Carta," retrieved from www.bl.uk/learning/timeline/item95692.html

Chapter 3: Walled Cities

p. 21, Reyerson, K. L. *The Art of the Deal: Intermediaries of Trade in Medieval Montpellier.* Leiden, Netherlands: Brill, 2001, p. 37.

p. 25, Janin, Hunt. *The University in Medieval Life, 1179-1499.* Jefferson, NC: McFarland and Company. Inc., Publishers, 2008, p. 61.

Chapter 4: Hearth and Home

p. 29, "Recognisance of a contract, London, 16 November 1308," retrieved from http://users.trytel.com/tristan/towns/florilegium/community/cmfabr01.html

p. 33, Matterer, James L. "A Boke of Gode Cookery." http://www.godecookery.com/godeboke/godeboke.htm.

Redon, Odile, Françoise Sabban, and Silvano Serventi. *The Medieval Kitchen: Recipes from France and Italy.* Translated by Edward Schneider. Chicago: University of Chicago Press, 1998.

Chapter 5: The City Community

p. 35, "Medieval Sourcebook: The Assizes of Bread, Beer, & Lucrum Pistoris," retrieved from http://legacy.fordham.edu/halsall/source/breadbeer.asp

p. 39, Hinds, Kathryn. *Venice and Its Merchant Empire.* Unpublished manuscript, 1997.

Chapter 6: A Center of Commerce

p. 41, "Medieval Sourcebook: The Regulations of the Weavers' Gild of Stendal, 1233," retrieved from http://legacy.fordham.edu/Halsall/source/1233Weavers4.asp

Chapter 7: An Urban Upbringing

p. 47, Orme, Nicholas. *Medieval Children.* New Haven, CT: Yale University Press, 2003, p. 141.

p. 50, Segar, Mary Gertrude. *A mediaeval anthology, being lyrics and other short poems, chiefly religious, collected and modernized.* p. 66-67, retrieved from https://archive.org/details/mediaevalantholo00sega

p. 53, Cosman, Madeleine Pelner. *Medieval Holidays and Festivals: A Calendar of Celebrations.* New York: Charles Scribner's Sons, 1981.

Chapter 8: Food and Festivities

p. 55, Jackson, Sophie. *The Medieval Christmas.* Gloucestershire, UK: The History Press, 2006.

p. 58–61, Chaucer, Geoffrey. *The Canterbury Tales: A Selection.* Edited by Donald R. Howard. New York: New American Library, 1969.

Chapter 9: Deadly Disasters

p. 63, *The Chronicle of William of Puylaurens: The Albigensian Crusade and its Aftermath,* trans. W.A. Sibly and M.D. Sibly (Boydell, 2003), retrieved from http://deremilitari.org/2014/03/the-siege-of-toulouse-in-1217-18-according-to-the-chronicle-of-william-of-puylaurens/

Bibliography

Alsford, Stephen. "Medieval English Towns." http://www.trytel.com/~tristan/towns/towns.html.

Blanchard, Laura V., and Carolyn Schriber. "ORB: The Online Reference Book for Medieval Studies." http://orb.rhodes.edu.

Chaucer, Geoffrey. *The Canterbury Tales: A Selection.* Edited by Donald R. Howard. New York: New American Library, 1969.

Chrétien de Troyes. *Le chevalier au lion (Yvain).* Paris: Librairie Honoré Champion, 1982.

Cosman, Madeleine Pelner. *Fabulous Feasts: Medieval Cookery and Ceremony.* New York: George Braziller, 1976.

———. *Medieval Holidays and Festivals: A Calendar of Celebrations.* New York: Charles Scribner's Sons, 1981.

Editors of Time-Life Books. *What Life Was Like in the Age of Chivalry: Medieval Europe AD 800–1500.* Alexandria, VA.: Time-Life Books, 1997.

Gies, Frances, and Joseph Gies. *Cathedral, Forge, and Waterwheel: Technology and Invention in the Middle Ages.* New York: HarperCollins, 1994.

———. *Life in a Medieval City.* New York: Harper Perennial, 1969.

———. *Women in the Middle Ages.* New York: Barnes & Noble, 1978.

Halsall, Paul, ed. "Internet Medieval Sourcebook." http://www.fordham.edu/halsall/sbook1.html.

Harbin, Beau A. C. "NetSERF: The Internet Connection for Medieval Resources." http://netserf.cua.edu/#Top.

Heer, Friedrich. *The Medieval World: Europe 1100–1350.* Translated by Janet Sondheimer. New York: World Publishing, 1962.

Herlihy, David, ed. *Medieval Culture and Society.* New York: Walker, 1968.

Herlihy, David. *Women, Family, and Society in Medieval Europe: Historical Essays, 1978–1991.* Oxford, UK: Berghahn Books, 1995.

Hinds, Kathryn. *Venice and Its Merchant Empire.* Unpublished manuscript, 1997.

Hoppin, Richard H. *Medieval Music.* New York: Norton, 1978.

Irvine, Martin, and Deborah Everhart. "The Labyrinth: Resources for Medieval Studies." http://www.georgetown.edu/labyrinth.

Luria, Maxwell S., and Richard L. Hoffman. *Middle English Lyrics.* New York: Norton, 1974.

Matterer, James L. "A Boke of Gode Cookery." http://www.godecookery.com/godeboke/godeboke.htm.

Milot, Marie-Christine. "Paris sous Philippe Auguste." http://www.philippe-uguste.com.

Packard, Sidney R. *12th Century Europe: An Interpretive Essay.* Amherst, MA: University of Massachusetts Press, 1973.

Redon, Odile, Françoise Sabban, and Silvano Serventi. *The Medieval Kitchen: Recipes from France and Italy.* Translated by Edward Schneider. Chicago: University of Chicago Press, 1998.

Shahar, Shulamith. *The Fourth Estate: A History of Women in the Middle Ages.* Translated by Chaya Galai. New York: Methuen, 1983.

Index

Page numbers in **boldface** are illustrations. Entries in **boldface** are glossary terms.